Writers Uncovered

TERRY PRATCHETT

Vic Parker

www.heinemann.co.uk/library
Visit our website to find out more information about Heinemann Library books.

To order:
☎ Phone 44 (0) 1865 888066
📄 Send a fax to 44 (0) 1865 314091
🖥 Visit the Heinemann bookshop at www.heinemann.co.uk/library to browse our catalogue and order online.

First published in Great Britain by
Heinemann Library, Halley Court, Jordan Hill,
Oxford OX2 8EJ, part of Harcourt Education.

Heinemann is a registered trademark of
Harcourt Education Ltd.

Editorial: Charlotte Guillain and Dave Harris
Design: Richard Parker and Q2A Solutions
Picture research: Hannah Taylor and
   Andrea Sadler
Production: Duncan Gilbert

Originated by Chroma Graphics (O) Pte Ltd.
Printed and bound in China by
   South China Printing Company

10 digit ISBN: 0 431 90633 5 (hardback)
13 digit ISBN: 978 0 431 90633 1

10 digit ISBN: 0 431 90643 2 (paperback)
13 digit ISBN: 978 0 431 90643 0

11 10 09 08 07
10 9 8 7 6 5 4 3 2 1

British Library Cataloguing in Publication Data
Parker, Vic
   Terry Pratchett. – (Writers uncovered)
   823.9'14
A full catalogue record for this book is
available from the British Library.

Acknowledgements
The publishers would like to thank the
following for permission to reproduce
photographs:
By kind permission Beaconsfield Library
p. **9**; By kind permission of Colin Smythe Ltd
on behalf of the Estate of Josh Kirby p. **19**;
By kind permission of Ian Oldroyd p. **42**;
Colin Smythe Ltd pp. **6, 16, 17, 27**; Corbis
pp. **21** (Peter Turnley), **4** (Rune Hellestad);
Empics/PA p. **37** (Michael Stephens);
Fremantle Media Ltd p. **38**; Mary Evans
Picture Library pp. **8, 20**; New Worlds
p. **12**; Orang-utan Foundation p. **23**;
Popperfoto.com p. **15**; Rex Features p. **13**
(Clive Postlethwaite); Rob Wilkins 2005 p. **24**;
Science Fantasy p. **11**; Topfoto.co.uk p. **10**;
Topham Picturepoint/PA p. **22**; Transworld
pp. **18, 29a, 29b, 29c, 31a, 31b, 31c, 33,
34, 35**; www.teacards.com p. **7**.

Very special thanks to Terry Pratchett for his
assistance in the preparation of this book.

CONTENTS

Words appearing in the text in bold, **like this**,
are explained in the glossary.

A RULE-BREAKING WRITER

Have you heard of a talking cat called Maurice or a time-travelling teenager called Johnny Maxwell? Have you come across two tiny but courageous nomes called Masklin and Grimma? They are all wonderful characters from the outstanding stories of Terry Pratchett.

Terry's writing breaks all the usual rules. His books do not appeal only to children or to adults, but to everyone. *Truckers* was the first children's story ever to appear in the adult paperback **fiction** best-seller lists in Britain. His stories cannot be grouped just as **science fiction** or as **fantasy**, because they are a brilliant mix of both. They are very funny, but through their humour they make many serious points about modern life and important issues. Terry's writing is simply unique.

This is the face behind the stories.

The brain behind the books

Terry has been one of the UK's best-loved authors for over 20 years and has millions of fans around the globe. He has written over 40 stories, which have been translated into more than 30 languages and have sold over 40 million copies worldwide.

There are Terry Pratchett clubs, magazines, websites, and **conventions**. There have been adaptations of his stories for radio, television, and the stage, and his books have inspired the production of computer games, models, audio books, quiz books, and even music CDs. Some people say Terry looks rather like one of the wizards that often appear in his stories. His writing is most certainly magic.

FIND OUT MORE...

Here are some of Terry's favourites:

Favourite book...	One of Terry's all-time favourite children's books is *Mistress Masham's Repose* by T.H. Wright. It is about a cruelly-treated orphan girl who is helped by Lilliputians – a race of tiny people from Jonathan Swift's classic novel, *Gulliver's Travels*.
Favourite animal...	Orang-utans. Terry once went out to their home in Borneo with a film crew and made a television programme about them.
Favourite plant...	Terry is fascinated by **carnivorous** plants. He has a greenhouse full of them!
Favourite interest...	Astronomy. Terry loves to study the universe and wonder about unknown worlds.
Favourite place...	His home, closely followed by any library.

Terry was born on 28 April 1948. His parents lived in a tiny village called Forty Green, near a town called Beaconsfield in Buckinghamshire. Terry's father, David, was a motor mechanic and his mother, Eileen, worked in the local post office.

Only, but not lonely

Terry was an only child, but he did not miss having brothers and sisters. Forty Green was so small that everybody knew each other. There were a few children the same age as Terry and they enjoyed going round in a gang together, exploring the lanes, fields and woods of the surrounding countryside. Terry also had grandparents in nearby Beaconsfield, whom he often visited. His grandmother was a well-educated woman, and was interested in books. His grandfather was a professional gardener who worked as a **groundsman** for a cricket club.

Beaconsfield is not far from London. Here Terry is on a day out in London's Trafalgar Square, feeding pigeons.

Exciting interests

As Terry grew up, he threw himself into one hobby after another. He grew very interested in electronics, and liked making crystal radio sets. With his dad, he built model rockets which could really lift-off. He also collected picture cards found in packets of Brooke Bond tea, on subjects like British birds and railway engines. His favourite subject was space. Terry became so fascinated by astronomy that his parents bought him his own telescope. He was captivated by the solar system and the stars.

Terry made his family drink a lot of tea so he could collect Brooke Bond picture card sets like this one.

OUT INTO SPACE

A series of 50 picture cards on Astronomy approved by A. Hunter, Ph.D. Secretary of the Royal Astronomical Society.

PRICE 6d.

FIND OUT MORE...

A crystal set is a simple type of radio you can make with just a few **components**, including a tin box, a length of wire, and a crystal such as galena. Many more people listened to the radio when Terry was a child than they do now. Television was still in its early days.

School days

Terry's first school was called Holtspur Primary. He did not like it much because he found school books boring and he was not good at lessons. At the age of nine, he was put in a class of pupils who were not likely to pass the entry exam for grammar school. However, around the same time, a family friend gave him a copy of *The Wind in the Willows* by Kenneth Grahame. Terry had no idea that books could be so enjoyable! He went from not wanting to read anything to being desperate to read everything. He started visiting the library, speed-reading his way through book after book, picking up all sorts of information and ideas. From then on, Terry often came top of his class.

Classic children's novel *The Wind in the Willows* is about the adventures of some riverbank and woodland creatures, including Ratty, Badger, Mole, and Toad.

Beaconsfield County Library was one of young Terry's favourite places.

Living at the library

Terry started spending so much time at Beaconsfield County Library that, by the age of ten, he had a Saturday job there. He stood on a stool to date-stamp the books being borrowed. The librarian issued Terry with lots of his own tickets, so he could take out as many books as he liked. No one guided Terry's reading. He dipped into the children's and adults' section, both fiction and **non-fiction**, as he liked.

Teenage years

Terry passed the **eleven-plus** entry exam for grammar school, but decided that High Wycombe Technical High School would suit him better. However, Terry found it just as uninspiring as his primary school. He felt that he learned much more at home from all the books he was reading. Apart from devouring all sorts of interesting information books, Terry loved fantasy stories – tales of imaginary, magical worlds and battles between the good and evil forces there. This led to a passion for ancient myths, legends, and folklore. Then Terry became hooked on science fiction. He once went to a convention for science-fiction fans and saw that the authors were just regular, normal-looking people. Terry realised that anyone could write wonderful stories. He started to wonder if he could also do it.

INSIDE INFORMATION

Terry later wrote a series of books about nomes called *The Bromeliad*. The end of this word sounds like "iliad", which is the name of a famous Ancient Greek story-poem.

This is a battle scene from Homer's *Iliad*.

A successful story

One day, when Terry was thirteen, an English teacher told his class to make up a short story. Terry wrote a science fiction tale called *The Hades Business*. It was so good he got full marks and it was published in the school magazine. Terry was thrilled. He sent it off to a science fiction magazine and, to his delight, they published it too! Terry was paid fourteen pounds, with which he bought a second-hand typewriter. His mum paid for him to have **touch-typing** lessons too. Terry was determined to write more stories.

No. 60
VOLUME 20
2/6
★
A Nova Publication
★
12th Year
of Publication

Science Fantasy

MERVYN PEAKE
An Appreciation by Michael Moorcock

e Dolphin and the Deep
IAS BURNETT CWANN

Terry's first story appeared in this edition of *Science Fantasy* magazine in 1963.

FIND OUT MORE...

Terry was good at art in a quirky, cartoony way. At school, he filled his notebooks with funny doodles. When he was in his mid-twenties, a few of his cartoons were printed in magazines. Several years later, Terry drew the illustrations for his first book.

Trash or treasure?

When sixteen-year-old Terry had taken his **'O' Level** exams, he stayed on at school to do A Levels. However, he still did not like school and thought that a lot of rules were stiff and silly. For instance, he once saw that some tattered old copies of the *Encyclopaedia Britannica* had been thrown into the dustbins. Terry and a couple of his friends thought they would still be interesting even if they were a little out of date, and they went to rescue them. The headmaster saw them and gave them a big telling off. The only thing Terry really enjoyed about school was being Deputy Head of the school library. Outside of school, his writing was going well. Terry had a second story, *Night Dweller*, accepted for publication by another magazine.

Terry's story appeared in this edition of *New Worlds* magazine in 1965.

A golden opportunity

Terry began wondering what he would do when he left school. He never dreamed of becoming a full-time writer, because very few people were good enough to make a living out of it. Terry had to find a job and write in his spare time. After a lot of thought, Terry decided he might like to be a **journalist**. He wrote to the editor of the local newspaper, the *Bucks Free Press*, to enquire about becoming a trainee in a year's time, after his A Levels. Unbelievably, there was a vacancy right there and then, and the editor offered it to Terry.

FIND OUT MORE...

Like Terry, nearly all best-selling authors start out doing other jobs. J.K. Rowling trained as a secretary, Philip Pullman was a teacher, and Michael Morpurgo was a soldier in the army.

Philip Pullman was a teacher in the historic city of Oxford.

Seventeen-year-old Terry left school and became a trainee reporter with the *Bucks Free Press*. He trained "on the job" in the busy newspaper office, and also went to college one day a week to take an A Level in English and a National Council for the Training of Journalists (NCTJ) qualification. One of the skills he learned was Pitman **shorthand**, so he could take accurate notes at top speed. Terry had to put in a lot of time at home studying, but he did not mind – his brain was well suited to journalism. When Terry sat his NCTJ exams, he came top in the country.

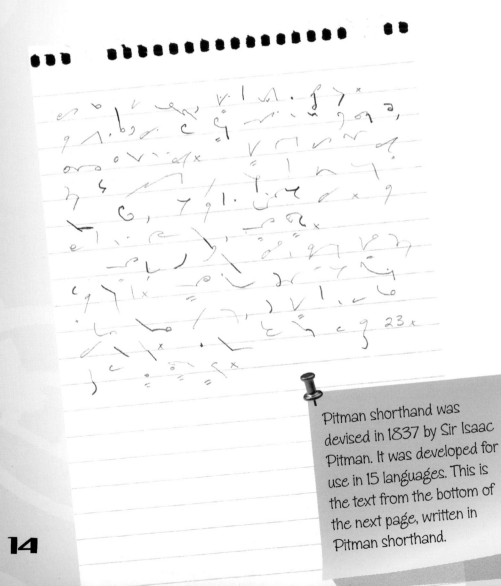

Pitman shorthand was devised in 1837 by Sir Isaac Pitman. It was developed for use in 15 languages. This is the text from the bottom of the next page, written in Pitman shorthand.

HAVE A GO

Ask a friend to read these pages aloud and see how quickly you can jot it down. Using Pitman shorthand, Terry could write over one hundred words a minute.

The offices that Terry worked in were like this, full of reporters working under pressure.

Terry's first book

As one of his duties on the newspaper, Terry had to write the children's page. He wrote a short story every Friday morning of about three hundred words, sometimes as part of a serial. Terry liked one particular serial so much that he reworked each episode at home into a longer version, until he had a full-length story. He sent it to a local publisher, Colin Smythe. Colin did not usually publish stories but he liked Terry's so much that he bought it. Colin's company was small and only printed a few books each year, so Terry had to wait for his story to be published. The book finally appeared when he was 23. It was called *The Carpet People*.

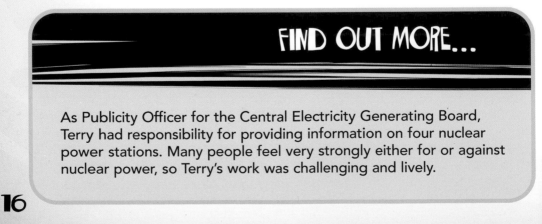

Here is Terry at the launch of his first novel, *The Carpet People*.

Making changes

Meanwhile, in 1968 Terry got married. He and his wife, Lyn, set up home in Somerset and Terry became a reporter with *The Western Daily Press*. Over the next few years, Terry returned to work on the *Bucks Free Press* as **sub-editor**, then went to the *Bath Evening Chronicle* as sub-editor and features writer. In 1976, the couple were delighted when their daughter, Rhianna, was born. And in 1980, Terry made one more big change to his life. He moved to a totally different job and became Publicity Officer for the Central Electricity Generating Board.

FIND OUT MORE...

As Publicity Officer for the Central Electricity Generating Board, Terry had responsibility for providing information on four nuclear power stations. Many people feel very strongly either for or against nuclear power, so Terry's work was challenging and lively.

Becoming a famous name

No matter where Terry was and what he was doing, he always made time to write stories. His second novel, *The Dark Side of the Sun*, was published in 1976 and his third novel, *Strata*, in 1981. They established him as a writer of hugely inventive, very funny stories that were a unique mix of science fiction, fantasy, and **parody**. Terry's fourth novel, *The Colour of Magic* (1983) was set on a planet which was a flat disc, which he called the Discworld. He rapidly wrote three further stories about the Discworld, and the series began to fly off bookshop shelves. Terry was offered a deal by a big publishing company to write six more books! He realised that he had the wonderful opportunity to give up his job and become a full-time writer.

The cover of *The Colour of Magic* showed readers the Discworld. The flat world sits on the back of four elephants standing on a turtle which is flying through space.

At first Terry found it strange not to have to get up and travel to an office to work. However, he relished having the whole day free to write – he did not want to spend time doing anything else. Colin Smythe became Terry's **agent**, taking on responsibility for the business side of things so Terry could concentrate on having ideas and making up new stories.

Books, books – and more books

Terry has now written over 30 Discworld books, involving a huge number of characters from humans to dwarves, dragons, and trolls. Some of the characters, such as the wizards from Unseen University and the City Watch guard, appear in more than one book. Death is the only character who appears in all of the books.

Here are Terry (on the left) and Colin (on the right) at a book publishing event.

The original paintings of the Discworld characters, such as this one of Death for the cover of *Soul Music*, were done by Josh Kirby.

The Discworld books are loved by readers of all ages, but Terry has written some especially for children: *The Amazing Maurice and his Educated Rodents* (2001), *The Wee Free Men* (2003), and *A Hat Full of Sky* (2004). Terry also wrote *The Bromeliad* especially for young people. It is a **trilogy** about a civilization of tiny nomes who cannot be seen by humans. He has written another trilogy about a young teenager called Johnny Maxwell, who finds himself saving aliens, helping dead people, and time-travelling.

Special skills

Terry brings endless ideas into his stories by including references to other books, writers and ideas. Sometimes these are obvious. For instance, *The Amazing Maurice and his Educated Rodents* is an instant contrast to the traditional folk story of *The Pied Piper of Hamelin*. Other times the references are harder to spot. For instance, the ancient philosopher Ptolemy, ancient Hindu myth-tellers, the Elizabethans, and a 1970s writer called Larry Niven all had ideas about how a planet could be flat and circular, like Terry's Discworld. This writing skill is called **allusion**, and Terry is a genius at enriching his stories with it.

INSIDE INFORMATION

Terry is also a master at using **satire** in his stories. Satirical writing thinly disguises real people and important issues, then pokes fun at them through humour, wit, and imagination.

In *The Pied Piper of Hamelin*, the piper is cleverer than the rats. In Terry's story, the rats are cleverer than the piper!

The Gulf War of 1990–1991 inspired Terry to write about war in *Only You Can Save Mankind*.

Thinking big

Terry often explores big ideas and serious issues. For example, the rats in *The Amazing Maurice and his Educated Rodents* wonder what happens to them when they die. Terry sometimes examines the concept of **organized religion**, such as by giving each society of nomes in *The Bromeliad* their own religious beliefs. Readers of Terry's books are also encouraged think about **prejudices**. For instance, in *Johnny and the Bomb* there are old-fashioned characters with prejudiced ideas about women and black people.

In his stories, Terry often looks at reasons for and against fighting. In *Only You Can Save Mankind*, he sets a computer-game war against the Gulf War in our own world. Terry also says that he originally wrote *The Carpet People* "in the days when I thought fantasy was all battles and kings. Now I'm inclined to think that the real concerns of fantasy ought to be about not having battles, and doing without kings..."

Finally, Terry loves to use exciting scientific ideas in his stories, such as the endless creation of other universes. In *The Carpet People*, the wise woman Culaina examines different futures and thinks: "all of them had to happen somewhere".

21

Being Terry Pratchett

Terry is now so famous and has so many fans all over the world, that it has become harder and harder for him to find time to write. He is always in demand to visit schools, attend book signings, and go to conventions and book tours abroad. Terry has sack-loads of fanmail every day and also receives hundreds of emails around the clock. These do not just come from fans, but also from editors, translators, and **publicists**. He often gets requests from young people asking for help with school projects!

Terry enjoys meeting his young readers.

Terry at home

Terry lives with Lyn in a beautiful 17th-century manor house, south-west of Salisbury. He says that one of the best things about being a best-selling author is that he can buy whatever books he wants, so he has a library in the main part of the house, another library in his study, and thousands more books. They are stored in boxes, heaped on the stairs, piled under beds and overflowing everywhere! He mostly enjoys reading non-fiction. Terry has also had an **observatory** built in his garden, so he can indulge his life-long interest in astronomy.

Terry donates the money he recives for public appearances to a charity that works to protect orang-utans, the Orang-Utan Foundation. One of the most popular characters in the Discworld books is an orang-utan librarian.

Terry gives money to help protect orang-utans in the wild.

TERRY'S WORK

When Terry first became a full-time writer, he was living in a smaller house where he worked in a spare bedroom. Then he had a bigger room built over his garage. Now, at the manor house, he has had a special building designed to be his writing room. He calls it "the Chapel", because it is made of stone and oak taken from an old chapel which once stood in the grounds. It has a huge south-facing window, so it is sunny and warm. Terry writes every day. It is the thing he loves doing most! He nearly always starts by half past nine in the morning because he works best before lunch.

Terry has a hi-tech computer system in his writing room.

Work in progress

Terry starts writing a story as soon as he has the basis of an idea. He never has the whole plot in his head or even much detail about characters – he begins writing to see what will happen and what the characters will be like. By the end of the first **draft**, Terry has told himself the story, although there are always bits that do not work too well, and he has new ideas all the time.

INSIDE INFORMATION

Terry thinks that everyone has good ideas for stories all the time. He says that while many people do not notice when they have an idea, he does. For instance, he was once playing a computer game called *Wing Commander* in which he had to shoot at aliens. He wondered what would happen if the aliens suddenly surrendered. He realised that this could be a great idea for a story, and started writing. Terry turned this idea into the book *Only You Can Save Mankind*.

Terry has the sort of mind that hangs on to odd facts and unusual information, so interesting bits and pieces are always popping into his head, sparking off new writing directions. Terry writes on a computer, so it is easy to make changes. He does lots and lots of rewriting before he is happy with a story.

Terry says that the way he writes is similar to how a painter builds up a painting. He does a rough sketch first, laying down hints of conversation, gradually bringing the outlines of characters into focus, and suggesting some background scenery. Then he goes over and over everything filling in detail, sometimes adding things, sometimes taking things away, dotting back and forth. He builds up layer after layer until finally, he stands back to look at his masterpiece!

THE CARPET PEOPLE

Main characters

Glurk.....................young chieftain of the Munrung tribe – a brave, strong warrior, although a little slow on the uptake

Snibril ....Glurk's younger brother – a bright, thoughtful lad

Pismire...................a shaman (holy man) and medicine man

mouls.....................villainous monster-men from the Unswept Regions who ride around on fierce snargs

Bane ....a Dumii General, an old friend of Pismire, and a moul-hunter

wights....................wise, mysterious people who look identical, have perfect memories, and a long tradition of strong religious beliefs and supersititions

Culaina ....a rare type of wight called a thunorg – she has the special power of knowing about all future possibilities

Brocando...............King of the Deftmenes, who was once enchanted into a statue

The plot

The Carpet is a perilous world of wool pile forests, earthed with dust and grit boulders, stretching from the Woodwall to the outermost fringes. It is habitat to all sorts of creatures, such as soraths, weft borers, gromepipers and termagants. It is also home to an empire of many different tribes and peoples, such as the Munrungs, the Deftmenes and the Dumii.

26

Now something terrifying is threatening the very existence of The Carpet: Fray is sweeping through the world, crushing towns and destroying cities. When their village is flattened, Glurk and Snibril have no choice but to set out on a perilous adventure into the unknown.

INSIDE INFORMATION

Terry wrote *The Carpet People* when he was seventeen years old. He drew some cartoon illustrations and a cover for it too. When he was 43, he revised the story and a different version was published. Terry's second version of the story is much more humorous, poking fun at would-be heroes and power-crazed rulers. He changed from using old-fashioned speech (such as "Greeting!") to modern (such as "Hello!"). He also turned a wise-man character called Culain into a wise-woman called Culaina. If you can get hold of both editions, see if you can spot more differences.

The Carpet People
Terry Pratchett

This is the first edition of *The Carpet People*, published in 1971. Terry drew the illustration for the cover himself.

TRUCKERS, DIGGERS, WINGS
(THE BROMELIAD TRILOGY)

Main characters

The Outsider nomes, including:
   Masklin .... a brave rat-hunter, the leader
   Grimma .... a plucky, determined young woman

Nomes of the Arnold Bros department store, including:
   **Angalo de
       Haberdasheri** ...... a brightly-coloured Duke's son
   **Dorcas del
       Icatessen** .... an elderly, stocky nome
   Gurder .... the Abbot's assistant and heir

The Floridian nomes, including:
   Shrub .... an old woman and the leader
   Topknot .... the chief warrior

Others:
   the Thing .... the Outsider nomes' sacred object
   Grandson Richard .. grandson of one of the brothers
                              who founded Arnold Bros.

The plots

Humans are unaware of nomes, tiny little people who live right alongside
them. In *Truckers*, one society of nomes live happily in a department store
called Arnold Bros., until they find it is about to be demolished. Luckily,
a small tribe arrive from the Outside – a place the nomes of the store
never before believed in – and help them escape.

In *Diggers*, the nomes think they have found a new home in the ruined buildings of an abandoned quarry. But when humans appear and the quarry is reopened, they are forced to fight for survival.

In *Wings*, the nomes come to believe that their rightful home is among the stars. But how will they travel into the sky? Maybe the answer lies in stealing Concorde…

INSIDE INFORMATION

The name of the trilogy, "bromeliad", is explained in *Diggers*. A bromeliad is a type of big flower that grows on a tree without taking any nourishment from it. It has leaves arranged in a bowl-shape, where some insects and small animals like frogs live as if in their own tiny world. So the word "bromeliad" represents the way the nomes live in the world of humans, but separately from them, while the world of humans is itself separate from the surrounding universe.

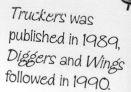

Truckers was published in 1989, *Diggers* and *Wings* followed in 1990.

THE JOHNNY MAXWELL TRILOGY
ONLY YOU CAN SAVE MANKIND,
JOHNNY AND THE DEAD, JOHNNY AND THE BOMB

Main characters

Johnny Maxwell..... the twelve-year-old hero
Wobbler Johnson,
   Yo-less, Bigmac,
   and Kirsty .... Johnny's friends
The ScreeWee........ a race of aliens inside a computer game
The Alderman,
   Mr Vicenti,
   William Stickers,
   Mrs Sylvia Liberty,
   Solomon Einstein,
   Mr Fletcher,
   and others .... the inhabitants of Blackbury cemetery
Mrs Tachyon........... a bag-lady who pushes around a
                      shopping trolley – which has the
                      power to travel through time

The plots

In *Only You Can Save Mankind*, Johnny Maxwell is fighting aliens in a computer game when something unexpected happens: the aliens surrender to him! To his shock, he now finds himself responsible for defending the race from the other humans playing the game, and helping them find a safe **extra-terrestrial** home.

In *Johnny and the Dead*, Johnny starts to see dead people in Blackbury graveyard. They have been disturbed by the news that the council have sold the graveyard to a development company for five pence, and they are not going to take it lying down!

In *Johnny and the Bomb*, Johnny discovers a magic shopping trolley which takes him and his friends back in time to 1941. They experience life in World War II, when bombs are dropping on their home town. Can Johnny and his friends change their history without altering their future?

INSIDE INFORMATION

Johnny is very different from a traditional hero. Normally heroes bravely rise to meet danger and strive to win honour and glory, even in the face of death. Johnny is a reluctant hero. He is forced into accepting a challenge and taking the lead. This is the case with many of the main characters in Terry's stories, from *The Bromeliad Trilogy* to the Discworld novels.

Only You Can Save Mankind was published in 1992, Johnny and the Dead in 1993, and Johnny and the Bomb in 1996.

THE DISCWORLD NOVELS

Main characters

The Amazing Maurice and his Educated Rodents

Maurice .... a smart-talking, streetwise cat

the educated
  rodents .... brave, talking rats, including: Hamnpork,
                        Darktan, and Peaches

Keith .... a boy who acts as Pied Piper

Malicia Grim .... daughter of the Mayor of Bad Blintz

Spider .... a monstrous rat king

The Wee Free Men and *A Hat Full of Sky*

Tiffany Aching .... our heroine, who lives at Home Farm
                         dairy, on The Chalk

Wentworth .... Tiffany's young brother

Roland .... the Baron's long-lost son

Miss Perspicacia
  Tick, Mistress
  Weatherwax,
  Miss Level .... experienced, famous witches

the toad .... Miss Tick's familiar – and Tiffany's helper

Queen of
  the Fairies .... ruler of a nightmarish magic kingdom

the Nac
  Mac Feegle .... blue-skinned, tiny creatures also known
                        as "the Wee Free Men", including: Rob
                        Anybody, Hamish, and Daft Wullie. Feegle
                        women, such as Fion and Jeannie, are rare...

THE AMAZING MAURICE AND HIS EDUCATED RODENTS

The plot

A boy teams up with a talking cat and a band of talking rats to fake the "Pied Piper" story as a means of making a living. They have considerable success – until they arrive in the town of Bad Blintz. Not only does a rather annoying girl realise what they are doing, but something very nasty is lurking in the cellars.

INSIDE INFORMATION

Malicia is obsessed with stories. She says that her grandmother and great-aunt were famous authors of fairytales – the Sisters Grim. This is an allusion to the Brothers Grimm, who in 1823 wrote down a collection of fairytales called *German Popular Stories*. The stories became some of the best-loved fairytales ever, such as *Hansel and Gretel* and *The Twelve Dancing Princesses*.

TERRY PRATCHETT
the Amazing Mau(R)ice
and his EDUCATED RODENTS
A STORY OF DISCWORLD

The Amazing Maurice and his Educated Rodents was first published in 2001.

THE WEE FREE MEN

The plot

Nightmares are turning up on the farm which is home to nine-year-old Miss Tiffany Aching, wannabe witch. To make matters worse, the Fairy Queen kidnaps Tiffany's younger brother. Tiffany sets off to rescue him, armed with only a frying pan for a weapon and her Grandma's book of magic. Fortunately, she has the help of a talking toad – and more importantly, an army of unpredictable "wee free men" in kilts called the Nac Mac Feegle.

INSIDE INFORMATION

Terry always creates many interesting female characters in his stories, but *The Wee Free Men* is the first in which women take over the action. Tiffany is one of the pluckiest and cleverest heroes in all of Terry's books. The Fairy Queen is chillingly cruel and controlling. The witches are extremely powerful. Even the ruler of the Nac Mac Feegle is a woman!

The *Wee Free Men* was first published in 2003.

TERRY PRATCHETT

the WEE FREE MEN

A STORY OF DISCWORLD

A HAT FULL OF SKY

The plot

Tiffany Aching is now eleven years old and beginning her apprenticeship in witchcraft. However, all is not going well. An unkillable spirit wants to take over her body. If Tiffany is going to stand a chance of defeating the mysterious menace, she needs the help of top witches Mistress Weatherwax and Miss Level, along with her old friends the Nac Mac Feegle.

INSIDE INFORMATION

The Nac Mac Feegle are pictsies, tiny creatures who were thrown out of Fairyland for being drunk and disorderly. Pictsies are much stronger than humans and also can move much faster, getting things done in double-quick time. Terry enjoys playing with ideas about time in his stories. The nomes of *The Bromeliad* are also quicker than us – they live at ten times the speed we do.

A Hat Full of Sky was first published in 2004.

TERRY PRATCHETT

A Hat Full of Sky

A STORY OF DISCWORLD

Terry's books have won or been **shortlisted** for countless top prizes and awards. Here are some of them:

- The Discworld novel *Pyramids* won the British Science Fiction Association (BSFA) Award.
- *The Amazing Maurice and his Educated Rodents* won one of the most prestigious honours in children's book publishing, the Carnegie Medal, in 2002. This is awarded by librarians to the best book of the year.
- *Truckers* was shortlisted for another major children's book award, the Smarties Prize.
- *Only You Can Save Mankind* was shortlisted for The Guardian Children's Fiction Award, *Johnny and the Dead* was shortlisted for the Carnegie Medal, *Johnny and the Bomb* was a Smarties silver medal winner and was also shortlisted for the Carnegie Medal and the Children's Book Award.
- *The Wee Free Men* won the WH Smith People's Choice Book Award in the Teen Choice category, and also the Locus Award for the Best Young Adult novel of 2003.

Terry has said that he is more proud to win awards for his children's books than for his adult ones. He has commented: "Writing for children is a lot harder than writing for adults, if you do it properly."

Special honours

The literary world holds Terry in high regard. He has been awarded an **honorary** degree called a Doctorate from not just one, but four universities. He has also served as the Chairman of the Society of Authors, and also of the panel of judges for a literary award for science writing called the Rhone-Poulenc Prize.

Royal approval

In 1998, the Queen honoured Terry for his outstanding work by choosing him for an award called the Officer of the Order of the British Empire. This means that Terry now has letters after his name: his full title is Terry Pratchett OBE. Terry went to Buckingham Palace to receive his OBE medal from the Prince of Wales.

A delighted Terry, after collecting his OBE medal from Buckingham Palace.

Another famous fantasy author who was once awarded a Queen's honour was J.R.R. Tolkien. He was given a CBE (Commander of the Order of the British Empire). Tolkien wrote *The Hobbit* and *The Lord of the Rings*, stories which had a big influence on Terry.

A scene from the animated television version of *Truckers*.

Adaptations of Terry's tales

Have you noticed that Terry's stories contain a lot of **dialogue**? One of his special skills is writing natural, lively conversation. This makes his stories particularly fun to read aloud, and several have been adapted for broadcasting on radio. The most recent version is the BBC's *Johnny and the Bomb*, released in 2006. *Truckers* was turned into animated film in 1992, and *Johnny and the Dead* was adapted as a television drama in 1995. Surely it is only a matter of time before one of Terry's stories is made into a major blockbuster movie.

Curtain up

Many of Terry's stories have been turned into stage plays by a specialist scriptwriter called Stephen Briggs. These include *Johnny and the Dead* and *The Amazing Maurice and his Educated Rodents*. Terry loves these play versions of his stories and finds the theatre very exciting because performances are live – anything can happen! There are always about 25 play versions of Terry's books in production in the world at any one time. Watch out for one at a theatre near you. The money the theatre companies pay Terry for permission to perform the plays all goes to The Orang-Utan Foundation.

HAVE A GO

If you wanted to perform a Terry Pratchett story as a play, which one would you choose? How would you change it from a book into a play script? Here are some things to think about:

- Break up your action and dialogue into scenes in different settings.

- Timescale – you could work from the beginning to the end or you could include "flashback" scenes of the past or "dream" scenes of the future.

- How will you tell your audience what the characters are thinking and feeling? Just through dialogue and action – or will you have a character who occasionally speaks directly to the audience, or a **narrator**?

- Try hard to make your characters' speech realistic and believable.

- Include in your script brief instructions to the actors how to move (for example, "he shrugs his shoulders") or speak their lines (for example, "in an angry voice").

- Suggest some special effects, stunts or music, if you want any!

Views in the news

Terry's novels have won praise from many critics, people who write their opinions of books for newspapers and magazines. Book reviews are important because they help readers decide whether to spend their time and money on a story or not. Here is an example of a review for *The Amazing Maurice and his Educated Rodents*, with some notes on how the critic has put it together. Would it encourage you to read the book?

Maurice looks like just another scruffy tomcat – until he starts speaking! There aren't many moggies who have their very own 'pied piper' and plague of rats either. And this is a plague of talking rats, who have the intelligence to read, reason and write. But Maurice and his fake-fairytale are about to meet their match in the town of Bad Blintz, where a terrifying evil lurks underground…

a little about the story without giving too much away

Terry Pratchett is the author of over forty best-selling stories for children and adults. *The Amazing Maurice and his Educated Rodents* is set on an imaginary planet called the Discworld, the scene of many other favourite Pratchett stories including *The Wee Free Men* and *A Hat Full of Sky*.

some background on the author

comparison with other works

This novel is an effortless, entertaining read, with brilliantly original characters and thought-provoking ideas. It was a worthy winner of the distinguished Carnegie Medal. Everyone over the age of nine will enjoy it, and it is of course a must-have for Pratchett's millions of existing fans worldwide.

the critic's opinion on whether it is a good or bad read, with clear reasons why

a recommendation of who the critic thinks will like the book

HAVE A GO

Why not try writing your own review of your favourite
Terry Pratchett book? You could give it to a friend who
does not know the book and see if they go on to read it.
Ask them to write a review back, recommending one of
their favourite books to you.

Pieces of praise

Here are some critics' opinions on Terry and his books:

"One of the best and funniest authors alive"
The Independent

"A writer with a masterstroke of imagination ... breaks all the boundaries between young and adult readership..."
The Daily Mail on The Carpet People

"Brilliantly funny dialogue, high peaks of imagination."
The Times on Truckers

"An impressively original book with its thrills and spills, its inventiveness, its wit . . ."
The Daily Telegraph on Only You Can Save Mankind

"Quite, quite brilliant!"
Starburst on The Wee Free Men

Terry has not taken a holiday for years because he loves being at home, writing. Besides, he regularly flies to America, Australia, New Zealand and other countries all over the world to promote his books and visit fans' conventions. At these events, Terry enjoys the chance to meet some of his biggest fans, who dress up as their favourite characters and chat all about his stories.

Future projects

Terry has worked with other writers on several books that are additional to his stories, such as illustrated versions of his tales, and new works such as *The Discworld Companion*, *The Science of Discworld*, and *Nanny Ogg's Cookbook*. Terry Pratchett fans just cannot get enough of his wonderful worlds, so there will be more of these extra-interest titles in future. Most importantly, Terry also has plenty of ideas for lots more stories!

Terry has signed thousands of books for his fans around the world.

Writing in focus

Here is what some of Terry's millions of fans think about him and his work:

"Everyone should read Terry Pratchett's stories – no matter what age."

Karen, aged 11, from Adelaide, Australia

"No one writes like Terry Pratchett – he's the greatest."

Graham, aged 12, from Cardiff, Wales

"Terry Pratchett rocks!"

Kurt, aged 13, from Detroit, USA

TERRY'S WISH LIST

Hopes...	Recently, Terry has been writing at the rapid rate of two books a year. He hopes he can learn to slow down and enjoy relaxing a little more.
Dreams...	Of having more hours in the day, to fit in everything he has to do and still have plenty of time for working on all his ideas.
Ambitions...	Terry is very happy with his life and all he has achieved with his writing. His ambition is to keep doing what he is doing for as long as possible – lucky for us!

TIMELINE

1948 Terry is born on 28 April. His family live in Forty Green, near Beaconsfield, in Buckinghamshire.

1957 A family friend gives Terry a copy of *The Wind in the Willows* by Kenneth Grahame, and Terry discovers the joy of reading.

1958 Terry has a Saturday job at Beaconsfield County Library.

1959 Terry goes to High Wycombe Technical High School.

1961 Terry writes a short story, *The Hades Business*, which is published in his school magazine.

1963 *The Hades Business* is published in a science fiction magazine called *Science Fantasy*. Terry buys a second-hand typewriter with the money he is paid and begins lessons to learn how to type fast.

1965 Terry has a story called *Night Dweller* published in *New Worlds* magazine.
After one year in sixth form, studying for A levels, Terry leaves school and becomes a trainee newspaper reporter on *The Bucks Free Press*. He also goes to college one day a week to continue studying for an A level in English and for his National Council for the Training of Journalists' (NCTJ) qualification.

1966 Terry writes a children's serial for the newspaper, which he reworks into a full-length novel, called *The Carpet People*.

1968 Terry gets married to Lyn.

1970 Terry and Lyn move to Somerset, where Terry works at *The Western Daily Press*.

1971 *The Carpet People* is published as a book by Colin Smythe.

1973 Terry begins to have cartoons he has drawn published in a magazine called *The Pyschic Researcher*.

1974 Terry begins work at the *Bath Evening Chronicle*.

1976 Terry and Lyn have a baby daughter, Rhianna.
Terry's second novel, *The Dark Side of the Sun*, is published.

1980 Terry becomes Publicity Officer for the Central Electricity Generating Board.

1981 Terry's third novel, *Strata*, is published.

1983 Terry's fourth novel, *The Colour of Magic*, is published.
This is the first of his stories to be set on the Discworld.

1987 Terry is offered an deal to write six more Discworld novels.
He gives up his Publicity Officer job to write full-time.
Colin Smythe, his former publisher, becomes his agent.

1989 *Truckers* is published and is shortlisted for the Smarties Prize.
The adult Discworld novel, *Pyramids*, is published and wins the
British Science Fiction Association (BSFA) Award.

1990 *Diggers* and *Wings* are published.

1992 A revised version of *The Carpet People* is published.
Only You Can Save Mankind is published and is shortlisted for
The Guardian Children's Fiction Award.

1993 *Johnny and the Dead* is published and is shortlisted for the
Carnegie Medal.

1996 *Johnny and the Bomb* is published. It wins a Smarties Prize Silver
medal and is also shortlisted for the Carnegie Medal and the
Children's Book Award.

1998 Terry is awarded an honour called an OBE from the Queen.

1999 Terry is awarded an honorary degree called a Doctorate from the
University of Warwick – three others follow from other universities.

2001 *The Amazing Maurice and his Educated Rodents* is published and
wins the Carnegie Medal.

2003 *The Wee Free Men* is published, winning the Locus Award for the
Best Young Adult Novel of the year and the WH Smith People's
Choice Book Award in the Teen Choice Category.

2004 *A Hat Full of Sky* is published.

FURTHER RESOURCES

More books to read

The Art of Discworld, Terry Pratchett and Paul Kidby (Gollancz, 2004)

The New Discworld Companion, Terry Pratchett and Stephen Briggs (Gollancz, 2004)

Audiobooks

Many of Terry's stories are also available as audiobooks on CD and cassette, including:

Truckers, *Diggers*, and *Wings* (ISIS Audio Books, 2004)

The Amazing Maurice and his Educated Rodents (Random House Children's Books, 2003)

The Wee Free Men (Random House Children's Books, 2003)

A Hat Full of Sky (Random House Children's Books, 2004)

The Carpet People (Random House Children's Books, 1997)

Websites

The publisher HarperCollins has a website about Terry:
www.terrypratchettbooks.com

Terry's publisher, Transworld, gives information on Terry:
www.booksattransworld.co.uk/terrypratchett

Probably the largest site by Terry's fans:
www.lspace.org

You can find out all about the Orang-utan Foundation:
www.orangutan.org

GLOSSARY

agent person who handles he business side of an author's work

allusion disguised reference to something else

carnivorous meat-eating

component part of a machine or piece of equipment

convention large meeting where fans of something or someone get together to enjoy events, displays, and guest appearances

dialogue conversation, speech

draft version of a piece of work before it is finished

eleven-plus special type of exam to get into selective schools

extra-terrestrial not on Earth, but in outer-space

fantasy story set in an imaginary, magical world

fiction imaginative writing, such as stories, rather than information writing

groundsman person who looks after a sports field

honorary something given to honour someone

journalist person who writes stories for newspapers

narrator person who tells a story

non-fiction information books, rather than made-up story books

observatory building specially designed to allow people to watch and examine the night sky

'O' level exam that is equivalent to a modern GCSE

organized religion large system of faith such as Islam, Christianity, Judaism, Sikhism, Hinduism

parody mimicking something in a funny way

prejudice opinion formed about someone or something without reason, knowledge, or experience

publicist someone whose job it is to tell the public about something such as a book or author

satire writing based on real people, events, and issues, to make fun of them in a clever, witty way

science fiction story based on science and technology but with made-up elements, often set in a different time or place

shorthand code that allows you to write down words as fast as people speak them

shortlist final list of candidates for an award, from which the winner is selected

sub-editor person whose job is to correct spelling, grammar, and punctuation

touch-typing skill of being able to type fast without having to look at the keys

trilogy series of three things which are related, for example stories using the same characters

INDEX